Little RIDDLERS

Little Poets

Edited By Byron Tobolik

First published in Great Britain in 2022 by:

Young Writers
Remus House
Coltsfoot Drive
Peterborough
PE2 9BF
Telephone: 01733 890066
Website: www.youngwriters.co.uk

All Rights Reserved
Book Design by Ashley Janson
© Copyright Contributors 2022
Softback ISBN 978-1-80459-200-7

Printed and bound in the UK by BookPrintingUK
Website: www.bookprintinguk.com
YB0522W

FOREWORD

Dear Reader,

Are you ready to get your thinking caps on to puzzle your way through this wonderful collection?

Young Writers' Little Riddlers competition set out to encourage young writers to create their own riddles. Their answers could be whatever or whoever their imaginations desired; from people to places, animals to objects, food to seasons. Riddles are a great way to further the children's use of poetic expression, including onomatopoeia and similes, as well as encourage them to 'think outside the box' by providing clues without giving the answer away immediately.

All of us here at Young Writers believe in the importance of inspiring young children to produce creative writing, including poetry, and we feel that seeing their own riddles in print will keep that creative spirit burning brightly and proudly.

We hope you enjoy riddling your way through this book as much as we enjoyed reading all the entries.

CONTENTS

Berkley First School, Berkley

Skye C (6)	1
Penny W (6)	2
Harri H (5)	3
Ottillie Mustow (7)	4
Bella Hoddinott (6)	5
Darcie Spain (6)	6
Phoebe Myring (6)	7
Phoebe W (6)	8
Oliver M (6)	9
Talulla P (6)	10
Edward D (7)	11

Blackshaw Lane Primary School, Royton

Mason Price (7)	12
Mahiul Haque (7)	13
Zunairah Ahmed (7)	14
Poppy Ward (7)	15
Erin Ward (7)	16
Matilda Hebblethwaite (7)	17
Ava Topping (7)	18
Mason Basnett (7)	19
Ava Jackson (7)	20
Gabriel Neto (6)	21
Molly Martin (7)	22
Freddie Pemberton (7)	23
Lewis Moss (7)	24
Elliemae Gibson (7)	25
Millie Sankey (7)	26
Reggie Lynch (8)	27
Lavinia Mannion (7)	28
Layton Jackson-Smith (7)	29
Isabelle Wills (7)	30

Emily Larner (7)	31
Joshua Collins (7)	32
Louie Childs (7)	33
James Deakin (7)	34
Lucas Buckley (7)	35
Tomos Heaword (7)	36
Noah Krupinski (7)	37
Kye Clarke (7)	38

Bryn Celyn Primary School, Pentwyn

Travis Francis (7)	39
Paisley Schaffer (7)	40
Mcauley Sanderson (7)	41
Keiron Parsons (7)	42
Tyler M (7)	43
Kathleen Moloney (7)	44
Logan Fish (7)	45
Lya Mahmood (7)	46
Wajd Alsawadi (7)	47

Fairview Community Primary School, Wigmore

Ekam Singh Chudha (8)	48
Poppy Gibson (8)	49
Ayaan Haseeb-Kaiser (7)	50
Jake Don (6)	51
Caitlyn Cowdry (10)	52
William Harnett (6)	53
Max Jewell (7)	54
Micaela Ward (7)	55
Florence Formoy (7)	56
Hugo McDonald-Smith (7)	57
Sofia Parker (6)	58

Lucy Hewkins (7)	59
Alana Broom (6)	60
Blake Sharkey (8)	61
Lucy Hewkins (7)	62

Glade Hill Primary School, Bestwood Park

Eric Turner (7)	63
Paisley Draycott (7)	64
Lamarne Edwards-Brown (7)	65
Aaliyah Msamba (6)	66
Leon Krasinski (7)	67
Logan Pattman-Wilson (6)	68
Billie Easom (7)	69
Leona Draper (7)	70
Scarlett Freeman (7)	71
Isabelle Pike (7)	72
Leah Norman (7)	73
Kaira Ococ (7)	74
Tahnia Mansaram-Hudson (7)	75
Lola Devlin (7)	76
Isabella Leivers (7)	77
Keegan Jackson (7)	78
Sansa Martin (7)	79
Logan Jackson (7)	80
Grace Kitwa (6)	81
Rosie Rike (7) & Freddie Proctor (7)	82
Olivia Marshall (7)	83
Cody Ford McKenna (6)	84
Kayde Wells (6)	85
Ethan Jones-Lake (7)	86
Bode Ajewole Anthony (6)	87
Codi Cannon (6)	88
Logan Newstead (7)	89
James Wade (7)	90
Kobie Ilett (7)	91
Agnes Racu (7)	92
Skyla-Mae Lockton (7)	93
Eliza Demi Beckford (6)	94
Oscar Barrass (6)	95
Matthew	96
Aliyah Maud (7)	97

Joseph Girling (6)	98
Oliver Joseph (6)	99
Cyrah-Rose Davis-Boulter (5)	100
Austin G (6)	101
Mya Gould (7)	102
Lacey Joy Tomlinson (6)	103
Freddie Jones (7)	104
Eli Church-Hanley (7)	105
Jacob Higgins (6)	106
Taylor Riley (6)	107
Joshua Bexon (6)	108
Elijah Edwards (6)	109
Kaelyn Belhadj (7)	110
Leah Bramley (6)	111

Killingholme Primary School, South Killingholme

Clara Smith (6)	112
Callie Hope (6)	113
Charleigh-Rose Hardy (6)	114
Charlie Douglass (6)	115
Isaac Hancock (6)	116
Riley Standley (6)	117
Raven Cornock (6)	118
Kane Stuart (6)	119

Lever Edge Primary Academy, Bolton

Nva Kawa (8)	120
Jake Pollitt (7)	121
Umar Mohammad (7)	122
Khadijah Hanna Hussain (7)	123
Faizaan Bharucha (7)	124
Maira Mahmood (7)	125
Zahra Azeem (7)	126
Sanah Omar (7)	127
Husna Mahamud (7)	128
Ameelia Safaa Mohamed (7)	129
Ayaan Mohammed (7)	130
Subhana Ibrahim (7)	131
Muhammed Ali Omar (7)	132
Hamza Ibrahim (7)	133

Mohammed-Adam Amir (7)   134

Nanaksar Primary School, Hillingdon

Aahana Chawla (6)	135
Prabaljodh Singh (6)	136
Praneesh Southeesan (6)	137
Dilsheen Nangpal (6)	138
Sienna Rana (6)	139
Gurmanbir Singh (6)	140
Anaya Chana (6)	141
Arshdeep Singh Bajwa (6)	142
Taranveer Singh (6)	143
Angad Randhawa (6)	144
Vinika Kaur (6)	145
Avneet Gurna (6)	146
Japji Dhillion (5)	147
Ashwika Logeswaran (6)	148
Sahibpreet Singh (6)	149
Fateh Singh (6)	150
Bhavik Bhavik (6)	151
Jugaad Singh Nagpal (6)	152
Anaya Sharma (6)	153
Harshaan Singh (6)	154
Vihaan Singh Bansal (5)	155
Zorawar Rana (6)	156
Arjun Singh Uppal (6)	157
Japleen Gulati (6)	158
Jayneev Kapoor (6)	159
Harjun Sira (6)	160
Harjaap Singh (6)	161
Arjan Singh Mann (6)	162
Aishleen Kaur (6)	163
Vicram Sandhu (5)	164

St Patrick's Catholic Primary School, Birmingham

Evnoia Shittu (5)	165
Ezer Gidey (5)	166
Morireoluwa Olusola (5)	167
Zanrae-Xya Arlington-Thompson (5)	168
Flourish Midele (5)	169
Michaela Dede-Bamfo (5)	170
Joy Segbedzi (5)	171
Havya Dhandapani (5)	172
Mateo Ramirez (5)	173
Elijah Ermias (4)	174

Westbourne School, Sheffield

Layla Allen (7)	175
Florence Smith (7)	176
Indu Shastry (8)	177
Beatrice Houston (7)	178
Rafe Dalrymple (7)	179
Edith Loncaster (7)	180
Grace Smith (7)	181
Zoya Qureshi (7)	182
Malakai Kurpiel-Wang (7)	183
Layla Horton (7)	184
Lucy Tallis (7)	185
Zayaan Aslam (7)	186
Patience Schofield (7)	187
Eva Loganathan (7)	188
Konstantina Oikonomou (6)	189

THE POEMS

Fluffy Friend

I have floppy ears.
I am nocturnal.
I hunt at night for my babies.
I am fluffy.
I have a brown body and yellow hair.
I am little.
I am so, so fluffy.
I have whiskers.
I hop and have floppy ears.
What am I?

Answer: A bunny.

Skye C (6)
Berkley First School, Berkley

Water Drops

I am squishy.
There are drops coming down.
I have drops coming down from me,
Especially when it's a little dark.
There are drops coming down from me.
What am I?

Answer: Rain clouds.

Penny W (6)
Berkley First School, Berkley

Soft Like A Pillow

I am blue and I sting.
I look like a pillow.
I have dots on me.
I have marks on my belly.
I am teal and I have a fin.
I live in the sea.
What am I?

Answer: A stingray.

Harri H (5)
Berkley First School, Berkley

Faster Than A Dog

I am an animal.
I have spots on my back.
I can run fast.
I have sharp teeth.
I eat meat.
You'll find me at Longleat drive-through.
What am I?

Answer: A cheetah.

Ottillie Mustow (7)
Berkley First School, Berkley

I Have A Water Splash

I am colourful.
I am hot.
I have water in me.
The water goes in the kettle to get hot.
You can paddle in me.
What am I?

Answer: A paddling pool.

Bella Hoddinott (6)
Berkley First School, Berkley

Harry

I eat tuna and fish.
I am silly and fluffy.
I can scratch.
I can cuddle.
I am small.
I have fluffy ears.
What am I?

Answer: A cat.

Darcie Spain (6)
Berkley First School, Berkley

Paw-Some!

I am fluffy all over.
I have four legs.
I am so warm with fluff all over.
People have to feed me twice a day.
What am I?

Answer: A cat.

Phoebe Myring (6)
Berkley First School, Berkley

Waddle, Waddle!

I am black and white.
I swim in the sea.
I eat fish.
I live in the sea.
I dive into the sea.
What am I?

Answer: A penguin.

Phoebe W (6)
Berkley First School, Berkley

Mr Kat

Sometimes I am big,
And sometimes I am little.
I live in the zoo.
I am soft.
What am I?

Answer: A meerkat.

Oliver M (6)
Berkley First School, Berkley

Something That I Love

I am bright.
I am yellow.
I come out in the summer.
I make people hot.
What am I?

Answer: The sun.

Talulla P (6)
Berkley First School, Berkley

The Howler

I howl at the moon.
I am black and grey.
I am fast.
I hunt for food.
What am I?

Answer: A wolf.

Edward D (7)
Berkley First School, Berkley

African Animal

I can be quite short and I can also be very long.
I can have a mix of colours.
I am very slippery.
I can glide around.
I can eat smaller animals.
I eat lots of food.
What am I?

Answer: A snake.

Mason Price (7)
Blackshaw Lane Primary School, Royton

African Animal

I am as small as a butterfly.
I have a very long tail.
I have two colours on my body.
Sometimes you will find me in the forest.
I have two hands.
I have no legs.
What am I?

Answer: A lizard.

Mahiul Haque (7)
Blackshaw Lane Primary School, Royton

My African Animal

I have four legs.
I have a small tail.
I have short legs.
I am black and white like a newspaper.
I have black stripes all over me.
I feel as tough as a rock.
What am I?

Answer: A zebra.

Zunairah Ahmed (7)
Blackshaw Lane Primary School, Royton

The Spotty Animal

I have four legs.
I have a white belly.
I have two horns.
I am spotty.
I have a line between my hooves.
I eat from the trees.
I have a long neck.
What am I?

Answer: A giraffe.

Poppy Ward (7)
Blackshaw Lane Primary School, Royton

My African Animal

I have an orange-yellow colour.
I have a long neck.
I have skinny legs.
I have curved ears.
You can ride on me.
I have two bumps on my back.
What am I?

Answer: A camel.

Erin Ward (7)
Blackshaw Lane Primary School, Royton

The Cute Baby

I am fluffy and cute.
I am related to a cat.
I have a medium-sized tail.
I have a little baby nose.
I have short ears.
I scamper quickly.
What am I?

Answer: A meerkat.

Matilda Hebblethwaite (7)
Blackshaw Lane Primary School, Royton

African Animal

I hunt very far.
I can hear very well.
I have blue eyes.
I feel like a French bulldog.
I look very scary.
I have a very fluffy tail.
What am I?

Answer: A hyena.

Ava Topping (7)
Blackshaw Lane Primary School, Royton

African Animal

I have a long tail.
I have four legs.
I have a fluffy head.
I have two round ears.
I am a carnivore.
I am the king of the jungle.
What am I?

Answer: A lion.

Mason Basnett (7)
Blackshaw Lane Primary School, Royton

My African Animal

I am a carnivore.
I have a long tail.
I am fluffy.
I am yellow like the sun.
I have a black pattern.
I look like a leopard.
What am I?

Answer: A cheetah.

Ava Jackson (7)
Blackshaw Lane Primary School, Royton

My African Animal

I have got sharp teeth.
I have short ears.
I have a short tail.
I have four fast legs.
I can climb trees.
I have whiskers.
What am I?

Answer: A jaguar.

Gabriel Neto (6)
Blackshaw Lane Primary School, Royton

African Animal

I am from the film Jumanji.
I have a long neck.
I have black feathers.
I have a beak.
I am very fast.
I can't fly.
What am I?

Answer: An ostrich.

Molly Martin (7)
Blackshaw Lane Primary School, Royton

African Animal

I am as small as a house brick.
I am in a little mob.
I am very curious.
I live in a burrow.
I am very cute.
I eat bugs.
What am I?

Answer: A meerkat.

Freddie Pemberton (7)
Blackshaw Lane Primary School, Royton

African Animal

I am as blue as the sky.
I can climb trees.
I am as fast as a cat.
I am smooth.
My head is yellow.
I have an orange tail.
What am I?

Answer: A lizard.

Lewis Moss (7)
Blackshaw Lane Primary School, Royton

Super Runner

I have a long tail.
I have short legs.
I have fortune cookie ears.
I eat meat.
I am spotty.
I am as fast as lightning.
What am I?

Answer: A cheetah.

Elliemae Gibson (7)
Blackshaw Lane Primary School, Royton

African Animal

I am black like the dark sky.
I have feathers.
My legs are skinny.
I have a long neck.
I can't fly.
I lay eggs.
What am I?

Answer: An ostrich.

Millie Sankey (7)
Blackshaw Lane Primary School, Royton

My African Animal

I am vicious.
I am as spotty as a dice.
I have two toes.
I am hairy.
I have straight knees.
I am orange and peach.
What am I?

Answer: A hyena.

Reggie Lynch (8)
Blackshaw Lane Primary School, Royton

African Animal

I have four legs.
I am big.
I am grey.
I have three nails on each foot.
I have floppy ears.
I have tusks.
What am I?

Answer: An elephant.

Lavinia Mannion (7)
Blackshaw Lane Primary School, Royton

African Animal

I have horns.
I have grey skin.
I have four legs.
I have one trunk.
I have floppy ears.
I eat grass.
What am I?

Answer: An elephant.

Layton Jackson-Smith (7)
Blackshaw Lane Primary School, Royton

African Animal

I am dotty like a giraffe.
I have two dark black eyes like a snake.
I have a short tail.
I have two small hands.
What am I?

Answer: A meerkat.

Isabelle Wills (7)
Blackshaw Lane Primary School, Royton

African Animal

I have four short legs.
I feel fluffy.
I live in the jungle.
I eat meat.
I am spotty.
I am sneaky.
What am I?

Answer: A leopard.

Emily Larner (7)
Blackshaw Lane Primary School, Royton

African Animal

I am like a leopard.
I am a carnivore.
I hunt prey.
I eat meat.
I am a fast animal.
I have a mane.
What am I?

Answer: A cheetah.

Joshua Collins (7)
Blackshaw Lane Primary School, Royton

African Animal

I have short legs.
I have a short tail.
I have a big body.
I have a big mouth.
I have sharp teeth.
What am I?

Answer: A hippopotamus.

Louie Childs (7)
Blackshaw Lane Primary School, Royton

African Animal

I have a long tongue.
I eat bugs.
I am invisible.
I am tiny.
I have a good grip.
I climb trees.
What am I?

Answer: A chameleon.

James Deakin (7)
Blackshaw Lane Primary School, Royton

African Animal

I am sneaky.
I have four legs.
I am a carnivore.
I can camouflage.
I can run fast.
I am spotty.
What am I?

Answer: A cheetah.

Lucas Buckley (7)
Blackshaw Lane Primary School, Royton

African Animal

I eat birds and mice.
I am a carnivore.
I eat eggs from nests.
I make nests.
I am naughty.
What am I?

Answer: A vulture.

Tomos Heaword (7)
Blackshaw Lane Primary School, Royton

African Animal

I eat meat.
I am yellow.
I can run fast.
I live in Africa.
I have long tusks.
What am I?

Answer: A sabre-toothed tiger.

Noah Krupinski (7)
Blackshaw Lane Primary School, Royton

African Animal

I have fur.
I have pointy ears.
I have a tail.
I have whiskers.
I have a mane.
What am I?

Answer: A lion.

Kye Clarke (7)
Blackshaw Lane Primary School, Royton

Scary Stinger

I can glow in the dark like a night light.
I have existed for 600 million years.
My mouth is in the centre of my body.
I can be clear like a fish tank.
I can be yellow like the sun.
Sea turtles hunt me.
I have tentacles that sting.
What am I?

Answer: A jellyfish.

Travis Francis (7)
Bryn Celyn Primary School, Pentwyn

The Best Anchor

I am a slow swimmer like a snail.
I am good at camouflage.
I have a flexible tail.
I hatch from eggs.
I have spikes on my back to protect me.
My spikes are sharp like scissors.
What am I?

Answer: A seahorse.

Paisley Schaffer (7)
Bryn Celyn Primary School, Pentwyn

Meat Eater

I am an apex predator.
I have tough skin.
I am a type of fish.
I have sharp teeth like a knife.
There are more than 500 different types of me.
I have an excellent sense of smell.
What am I?

Answer: A shark.

Mcauley Sanderson (7)
Bryn Celyn Primary School, Pentwyn

Scary Predator

I am grey and blue.
I have 300 teeth.
There are 500 different types of me.
My teeth are sharp like a knife.
I have an excellent sense of smell.
I lose and replace my teeth.
What am I?

Answer: A shark.

Keiron Parsons (7)
Bryn Celyn Primary School, Pentwyn

Snippy Sidewalker

I am yellow like the sun.
I am an omnivore.
I have a hard shell to protect me.
My pincers are sharp like scissors.
I lay up to 100,000 eggs.
I have ten legs.
What am I?

Answer: A crab.

Tyler M (7)
Bryn Celyn Primary School, Pentwyn

Clever Creature

I am good at camouflage.
I have eight tentacles.
I am a carnivore.
I have three brains.
I squirt black ink when I am scared.
What am I?

Answer: An octopus.

Kathleen Moloney (7)
Bryn Celyn Primary School, Pentwyn

High Jumper

I swim fast.
I am smooth.
I am clever.
I use my blowhole to breathe.
I am a mammal.
I live in tropical oceans.
What am I?

Answer: A dolphin.

Logan Fish (7)
Bryn Celyn Primary School, Pentwyn

Fast Swimmer

I am smooth.
I am friendly.
I am grey.
I jump out of the water.
I am clever.
I live in tropical oceans.
What am I?

Answer: A dolphin.

Lya Mahmood (7)
Bryn Celyn Primary School, Pentwyn

Fast Swimmer

I am smooth.
I am big.
I am blue.
I am clever.
I am a mammal.
I have a pointy nose.
What am I?

Answer: A dolphin.

Wajd Alsawadi (7)
Bryn Celyn Primary School, Pentwyn

Wondrous Ball

You'll find me in a white and blue ball.
You will find me in a magical land.
You will find me near the ocean.
You will find me in a shell.
You will find me with a trainer.
You will find me blowing bubbles.
Who am I?

Answer: Squirtle.

Ekam Singh Chudha (8)
Fairview Community Primary School, Wigmore

Brain Freezer

I am icy cold.
I am your favourite treat.
I give you brain freeze from your head to your feet.
I can be red or blue, or a mixture of the two.
I am crunchy at first, but if you leave me too long, I will be all wet.
What am I?

Answer: A slushy.

Poppy Gibson (8)
Fairview Community Primary School, Wigmore

Hunger Express

I burn your tastebuds.
When you eat me, you beg for more.
When you taste me, your tongue is on fire.
I am as orange as a tiger.
I am as chewy as a piece of meat.
What am I?

Answer: Morley's Chicken Wing.

Ayaan Haseeb-Kaiser (7)
Fairview Community Primary School, Wigmore

Avocado Planter

I only eat leaves in my lifetime.
I am blind.
I only leave my tree for a poo or wee.
It takes me 20 minutes to cross a motorway.
One of South America's greatest climbers.
What am I?

Answer: A sloth.

Jake Don (6)
Fairview Community Primary School, Wigmore

The Death Creature

My blood is as cold as an icicle.
My skin is as rough as bark.
You better not come near me,
Or I'll bite your head apart.
My colour acts as good camouflage.
What am I?

Answer: A crocodile.

Caitlyn Cowdry (10)
Fairview Community Primary School, Wigmore

Night-Time Visitor

My spikes are as sharp as a knife.
I am a night-time omnivore.
My habitat is in danger.
You will find me snuffling on the floor.
I have the cutest little face.
What am I?

Answer: A hedgehog.

William Harnett (6)
Fairview Community Primary School, Wigmore

A Plate Of Wiggles

I am best friends with a meatball.
I am wiggly like a worm.
I get sucked up.
I live with a ball.
With a suck and a slurp,
It leads to a very big burp.
What am I?

Answer: Spaghetti.

Max Jewell (7)
Fairview Community Primary School, Wigmore

The Bun

I can be delivered by bike or by car.
I start with an M.
I am tasty and delicious.
You can eat me.
I am open at weekends and after school.
What am I?

Answer: McDonald's.

Micaela Ward (7)
Fairview Community Primary School, Wigmore

Fields Of Red

We are black, red and green.
We are remembered on Remembrance Day.
We remind you of the fallen.
Our best month is November.
We are good gifts.
What are we?

Answer: Poppies.

Florence Formoy (7)
Fairview Community Primary School, Wigmore

Mystery Boarder

I ride up high.
I sometimes get wiped out.
I have a board.
I need wax to grip.
I sometimes lay on my board.
Beware of the weever fish.
What am I?

Answer: A surfer.

Hugo McDonald-Smith (7)
Fairview Community Primary School, Wigmore

The Icy Meltdown

You find me in Asia.
They sparkle in the sun.
You dig them up from the dirt.
They are mostly white.
But look closer for a delight.
What am I?

Answer: A diamond.

Sofia Parker (6)
Fairview Community Primary School, Wigmore

Icy Meltdown

I melt in the sun.
I am all different flavours.
I am big or small.
I am juicy and fun.
I drip everywhere if you leave me too long.
What am I?

Answer: Ice cream.

Lucy Hewkins (7)
Fairview Community Primary School, Wigmore

Girl's Best Friend

It shines in the sun.
It can be different colours.
You find them in the mud.
They are sparkly.
People like to wear them.
What is it?

Answer: A diamond.

Alana Broom (6)
Fairview Community Primary School, Wigmore

The Horned Wonder

I have a small tail and my horns are sharp.
My loud voice sounds nothing like a harp.
My hard hooves mean I can jump on roofs.
What am I?

Answer: A goat.

Blake Sharkey (8)
Fairview Community Primary School, Wigmore

The King Of The Jungle

I am the king of the jungle!
I do a big roar!
I have a gorgeous piece of hair.
I eat meat a lot.
I run extra fast.
What am I?

Answer: A lion.

Lucy Hewkins (7)
Fairview Community Primary School, Wigmore

The Breezy State Of The USA

I am the largest state in the USA.
I am the most northern state in the USA and I've even got a territory in the Arctic Circle.
I've got two massive peninsulas and it's due to continental drift.
I make the USA have two borders with the maple leaf.
I am the 49th state of the USA and became a state in 1959.
What state am I?

Answer: Alaska.

Eric Turner (7)
Glade Hill Primary School, Bestwood Park

A Common Pet

I like to sleep because it helps me rest.
I normally live in the alley.
I have something on my face, they're called whiskers.
I have something on my head, they're tall ears that help me to hear my prey.
I eat fish because they're slimy.
I climb trees because I have claws.
What am I?

Answer: A cat.

Paisley Draycott (7)
Glade Hill Primary School, Bestwood Park

King Of The Lake

I am a killer, I love to feed on people.
I am in a group of killers in a lake.
I eat meat all day.
I am not friendly to people.
I am not friendly to children or adults.
I will kill you if I see you.
I have got a long jaw.
I snap.
I am not to be kept as a pet.
What am I?

Answer: A crocodile.

Lamarne Edwards-Brown (7)
Glade Hill Primary School, Bestwood Park

The Deep Sea Creature

I am peaceful.
I go in the water and sometimes I go on the sand, but not for too long.
I have got no teeth.
I am not scary.
I do not eat any of you.
I am mostly big, but sometimes I am small.
I don't normally go down into the deep sea, I am normally on top of the sea.
What am I?

Answer: A turtle.

Aaliyah Msamba (6)
Glade Hill Primary School, Bestwood Park

The Fluffy Night Hunter

I have a beak that has a sharp, pointy end so that my prey can't slide out.
I am a nocturnal animal.
I can see in the dark so I can easily catch my prey.
I have strong, fluffy wings.
I have a round or heart-shaped head.
I sometimes steal other birds' abandoned nests.
What am I?

Answer: An owl.

Leon Krasinski (7)
Glade Hill Primary School, Bestwood Park

One Dead, One Alive

One of me is alive and one of me is dead.
One keeps us alive and one does not.
One of me eats spheres.
One of me is a sphere made of gas.
One of me is big and one is small.
I can change from one to the other.
What am I?

Answer: *The sun and a black hole.*

Logan Pattman-Wilson (6)
Glade Hill Primary School, Bestwood Park

The Spotty Yellow Animal

I am a light yellow colour.
I have black spots on my back.
I have a long, large neck.
I like to drink fresh, cold water.
I live in the zoo and in safari parks with other animals.
I have four long, spotty legs.
What am I?

Answer: A giraffe.

Billie Easom (7)
Glade Hill Primary School, Bestwood Park

The Kind, White Animal

I have white fur and live with a family.
I can be male or female.
I am as white as the clouds in the sky.
I have medium-sized pointy ears.
I can have puppies and I sleep with them.
I like to play with children.
What am I?

Answer: A dog.

Leona Draper (7)
Glade Hill Primary School, Bestwood Park

My Noisy Animal

A group of me is called a herd.
I can't live in hot places.
I love to drink fresh clean water.
I eat grass, apples and hay.
I can have different coloured fur.
I can be a cob, pony or a shetland.
What am I?

Answer: A horse.

Scarlett Freeman (7)
Glade Hill Primary School, Bestwood Park

The Kind Woman

I am nearly in my 60s.
I am retiring in a few weeks so I can relax at home.
Children think I am enthusiastic and beautiful.
I have worked for many years.
I have short hair but not too short.
Who am I?

Answer: Mrs Bucksten.

Isabelle Pike (7)
Glade Hill Primary School, Bestwood Park

The Animal Eater

I hunt during the night.
I am always ready to snap at animals.
I eat other animals.
I am furry.
I am fiery orange.
I have a white belly.
I am not a nice animal,
And you cannot adopt me.
What am I?

Answer: A fox.

Leah Norman (7)
Glade Hill Primary School, Bestwood Park

The Hidden High

I fly up into the beautiful air.
I am somewhere calm and green.
I am always sitting somewhere.
I am so colourful like a rainbow.
I only have two legs.
I always lick my beautiful, black beak.
What am I?

Answer: A parrot.

Kaira Ococ (7)
Glade Hill Primary School, Bestwood Park

Reflections

I help a part of your body and stop it from hurting.
I am essential in a type of season.
I smell sweaty and wet sometimes.
I get used because I help people.
I get used a lot during the summer.
What am I?

Answer: Sunglasses.

Tahnia Mansaram-Hudson (7)
Glade Hill Primary School, Bestwood Park

A Hopping Mammal

I can hop really high.
I have different coloured fur on my body.
I live in the grass or holes underground.
I have long, floppy ears.
I have four short legs.
I can be a pet.
What am I?

Answer: A bunny.

Lola Devlin (7)
Glade Hill Primary School, Bestwood Park

A Large Herbivore

I have a long neck.
I eat lettuce, grass and fruit.
I sleep at night.
I can live in the zoo or in safari parks.
I have a black tongue.
I have brown spots on my body.
What am I?

Answer: A giraffe.

Isabella Leivers (7)
Glade Hill Primary School, Bestwood Park

The Rolling Machine

I have a round, hard surface.
I can get kicked super hard.
I am very, very old.
I can roll but I have no legs.
I get kicked by pros.
I have no vertices or corners.
What am I?

Answer: A football.

Keegan Jackson (7)
Glade Hill Primary School, Bestwood Park

Long Neck

I have a black tongue to eat plants.
I am a herbivore.
I have long legs to run.
I am a female.
I have soft, brown spots.
Lions like to chase me so they can eat me.
What am I?

Answer: A giraffe.

Sansa Martin (7)
Glade Hill Primary School, Bestwood Park

The Hard-Scaled Reptile

I have four legs that are long.
I eat insects that are alive.
I like to hide in my cave.
I like trying to get out of my cave.
If you take me out, be careful.
What am I?

Answer: A bearded dragon.

Logan Jackson (7)
Glade Hill Primary School, Bestwood Park

Frozen And Free

They come down at Christmas.
They are frozen.
You see them in the movie, Frozen.
They have sharp points.
They are icy.
They fall softly through the air.
What are they?

Answer: Snowflakes.

Grace Kitwa (6)
Glade Hill Primary School, Bestwood Park

The Fantastic Machine

A human controls me.
I have circles for legs.
I come in different colours.
I have doors so people can get in me.
I am made of metal.
I have oil instead of water.
What am I?

Answer: A car.

Rosie Rike (7) & Freddie Proctor (7)
Glade Hill Primary School, Bestwood Park

My Fluffy Animal

I can be male or female.
I can perform lots of tricks.
I can jump really high.
I can be a pet.
I am a Chihuahua mixed with a Jack Russell.
My name is Buddy.
What am I?

Answer: A dog.

Olivia Marshall (7)
Glade Hill Primary School, Bestwood Park

Spiky Beast

I am spiky.
I am a meat eater.
I am a type of lizard.
I have a long tail.
I live in Madagascar.
I love the heat.
I am orange and yellowish.
What am I?

Answer: A bearded dragon.

Cody Ford McKenna (6)
Glade Hill Primary School, Bestwood Park

The Slitherer

I am born in an egg.
I am not so big.
I eat birds' eggs.
I breathe air.
I smell using my tongue.
I am not so fast.
I don't have legs.
What am I?

Answer: A snake.

Kayde Wells (6)
Glade Hill Primary School, Bestwood Park

The Ocean Killer

It doesn't like anyone near it.
Its teeth are sharper than a knife.
It zooms like a flash in the dark.
It will eat anyone smaller than itself.
What is it?

Answer: A shark.

Ethan Jones-Lake (7)
Glade Hill Primary School, Bestwood Park

Like A White Bird

I can fly.
I make your head hurt sometimes.
I am white.
I see the clouds and the sun.
I see the sky.
In the end, I go to countries.
What am I?

Answer: An aeroplane.

Bode Ajewole Anthony (6)
Glade Hill Primary School, Bestwood Park

The Beautiful Sky

I am beautiful and colourful in the sky.
I am lots of colours in the rain and sun.
I am with the clouds in the air.
I fill you with happiness.
What am I?

Answer: A rainbow.

Codi Cannon (6)
Glade Hill Primary School, Bestwood Park

The Human Swing

I shoot sticky webs.
I am a superhero.
I am from Marvel.
I have a red suit.
I have black stripes.
I save people who are in danger.
Who am I?

Answer: *Spider-Man.*

Logan Newstead (7)
Glade Hill Primary School, Bestwood Park

The Happy Tail Wagger

I can be a cuddly pet.
I like to chase the bouncy ball.
You can take me for a walk.
I love the smell of chicken.
Can you give me some toys?
What am I?

Answer: A dog.

James Wade (7)
Glade Hill Primary School, Bestwood Park

The Four-Legged Object

I have four legs.
I am made out of wood and plastic.
I have screws in me.
I have pillows on me and a blanket.
People read books on me.
What am I?

Answer: A chair.

Kobie Ilett (7)
Glade Hill Primary School, Bestwood Park

What Am I?

I have long, pointy ears.
I hop all around.
I eat tasty carrots.
I have fluffy fur.
I sleep during the night.
I can be a pet.
What am I?

Answer: A rabbit.

Agnes Racu (7)
Glade Hill Primary School, Bestwood Park

A Very Friendly Animal

I live in a group called a pack.
I can be a pet.
I love to eat treats.
I love to play with humans.
I can have babies called puppies.
What am I?

Answer: A dog.

Skyla-Mae Lockton (7)
Glade Hill Primary School, Bestwood Park

Howdy, Cowboy!

I am a toy.
I am in a movie.
I ride on Bullseye.
I have a star.
I have cowboy shoes.
I have a cowboy hat.
Who am I?

Answer: Woody from Toy Story.

Eliza Demi Beckford (6)
Glade Hill Primary School, Bestwood Park

A Fire-Breather

I can breathe fire.
I can be hot on the inside.
I have four legs.
I live near a volcano.
I have wings.
I can fly.
What am I?

Answer: A dragon.

Oscar Barrass (6)
Glade Hill Primary School, Bestwood Park

Fast Teeth

It has sharp teeth and claws.
It scratches.
It likes to sleep.
The bad ones are white.
It likes to clean itself.
What is it?

Answer: A cheetah.

Matthew
Glade Hill Primary School, Bestwood Park

The Flat, Brown Object

I have four legs to keep me standing.
I am flat so you can rest on me.
I am a rectangle.
You can put your dinner on me.
What am I?

Answer: A table.

Aliyah Maud (7)
Glade Hill Primary School, Bestwood Park

Big, Bad And Red

I have wings.
My ears are sharp.
My teeth are sharp.
I have got big feet.
I am hot inside.
I breathe fire.
What am I?

Answer: A dragon.

Joseph Girling (6)
Glade Hill Primary School, Bestwood Park

The Fast Runner

Sometimes I eat people.
I am mean.
I have sharp teeth.
I live in the jungle.
I am very fast.
I am black.
What am I?

Answer: A puma.

Oliver Joseph (6)
Glade Hill Primary School, Bestwood Park

Night-Time Animal

It is black.
It comes out at night.
It is small.
Its mouth is small.
It eats fruit.
It lives in a cave.
What is it?

Answer: A bat.

Cyrah-Rose Davis-Boulter (5)
Glade Hill Primary School, Bestwood Park

Hot Flames

I am the hottest thing on Earth.
I can cook your dinner.
I start with the letter F.
I can burn you.
I am hot.
What am I?

Answer: Fire.

Austin G (6)
Glade Hill Primary School, Bestwood Park

A Hard-Shelled Creature

I have a green, hard shell.
I am really slow.
I can swim in the deep, blue ocean.
You can keep me as a pet.
What am I?

Answer: A turtle.

Mya Gould (7)
Glade Hill Primary School, Bestwood Park

Fast Beast

I eat meat.
I am sneaky.
I have spots.
I roar but sometimes I purr.
I have whiskers.
I am fast.
What am I?

Answer: A cheetah.

Lacey Joy Tomlinson (6)
Glade Hill Primary School, Bestwood Park

The Metal Man

I serve you drinks and food.
I help you with things.
I drink oil and fall over.
I can't swim or eat.
What am I?

Answer: A robot.

Freddie Jones (7)
Glade Hill Primary School, Bestwood Park

A Roaring Purr

I roar.
I eat meat.
I scare people.
I am the king of the jungle.
I live in the wild.
I fight.
What am I?

Answer: A lion.

Eli Church-Hanley (7)
Glade Hill Primary School, Bestwood Park

Meat Eater

I roar.
I live in the wild.
I eat meat.
I am furry.
I like water.
I don't eat people.
What am I?

Answer: A tiger.

Jacob Higgins (6)
Glade Hill Primary School, Bestwood Park

Cool Snack

You can eat me.
You can lick me.
I come in a truck.
I come in the summer.
I have a cone.
What am I?

Answer: Ice cream.

Taylor Riley (6)
Glade Hill Primary School, Bestwood Park

Big, Bad And Red

It is big.
It can fly.
It is brave.
It is fast.
It is tall.
Its teeth are sharp.
What is it?

Answer: A dragon.

Joshua Bexon (6)
Glade Hill Primary School, Bestwood Park

The Hopping Beast

I jump.
I hop.
I have big ears.
I run.
I live in the forest.
I have four legs.
What am I?

Answer: A rabbit.

Elijah Edwards (6)
Glade Hill Primary School, Bestwood Park

Kitchen Whizz

I work at night.
I wear a white uniform.
I use lots of ingredients.
I work extremely hard.
What am I?

Answer: A chef.

Kaelyn Belhadj (7)
Glade Hill Primary School, Bestwood Park

A Daytime Animal

It is grey.
It has four legs.
It has big ears.
What is it?

Answer: An elephant.

Leah Bramley (6)
Glade Hill Primary School, Bestwood Park

Hop, Hop!

I have a fluffy tail.
I eat orange carrots and drink water.
I live in the wild but you can have me as a pet.
I hop around but if you scare me, I will hide in a hole.
As a baby, I am called a kitten.
What am I?

Answer: A bunny rabbit.

Clara Smith (6)
Killingholme Primary School, South Killingholme

Whiskers And Milk

I have three long whiskers.
I drink milk and eat tuna.
I live in the wild but you can have me as your pet.
I can climb trees of any size.
I can be tabby or ginger.
People say that I don't like dogs.
What am I?

Answer: A cat.

Callie Hope (6)
Killingholme Primary School, South Killingholme

Hoppity Hop

I have big, fluffy ears.
My favourite food is orange.
I live in the forest.
I hop around in the forest.
I have two little teeth sticking out.
When I was a baby, I was a kitten.
What am I?

Answer: A bunny rabbit.

Charleigh-Rose Hardy (6)
Killingholme Primary School, South Killingholme

The Big Cat

I am a carnivore.
I have orange and black stripes.
I live in the jungle.
I run faster than an elephant.
I have long, sharp claws.
You won't want to meet me.
What am I?

Answer: A tiger.

Charlie Douglass (6)
Killingholme Primary School, South Killingholme

As Fast As Lightning

I have four red wheels.
People watch me on TV.
I am faster than lightning.
Somebody sits inside me.
Watch me on a Sunday.
We are having a race.
What am I?

Answer: An F1 racing car.

Isaac Hancock (6)
Killingholme Primary School, South Killingholme

Snap! Snap!

I have green scales.
I go snap with my sharp teeth.
I can swim.
I move slowly but snap quickly.
I can go underwater.
You can visit me at the zoo.
What am I?

Answer: A crocodile.

Riley Standley (6)
Killingholme Primary School, South Killingholme

Fluffy Ears And Sharp Claws

I have fluffy ears.
I drink milk.
I live in a house.
My eyes are blue and shiny.
I can run fast and climb trees.
My teeth are sharp.
What am I?

Answer: A cat.

Raven Cornock (6)
Killingholme Primary School, South Killingholme

The Big, Fluffy Mane

I have sandy, yellow fur.
I am a carnivore.
I live in the jungle.
I sneak up on my prey.
I am the king.
Sometimes I eat fish.
What am I?

Answer: A lion.

Kane Stuart (6)
Killingholme Primary School, South Killingholme

Where Is It?

There are countless jobs there.
Many people visit throughout the summer.
There are several yachts.
Surfing is popular there.
You must apply sunscreen there.
There are multiple seashells.
Where is it?

Answer: The seaside.

Nva Kawa (8)
Lever Edge Primary Academy, Bolton

It's Not One Word

What has four letters but sometimes has nine?
Read the first and sixth words.
What does have four letters but sometimes has nine.
What will happen?
Sometimes it happens.
What am I?

Answer: What and Sometimes.

Jake Pollitt (7)
Lever Edge Primary Academy, Bolton

What Is It?

Its teeth are as sharp as a shark,
And its teeth are strong.
It's a mammal.
Its teeth can bite through bone.
It has stripes like a zebra.
It wakes up at night.
What is it?

Answer: A Tasmanian devil.

Umar Mohammad (7)
Lever Edge Primary Academy, Bolton

What Am I?

I am white like a polar bear.
I can hop and jump.
I have sharp teeth.
I often come in the colour white.
I have whiskers but I am not a cat.
I have five letters in my name.
What am I?

Answer: A bunny.

Khadijah Hanna Hussain (7)
Lever Edge Primary Academy, Bolton

What Is It?

You go there in the summer.
The temperature is 20 degrees.
You must put sun cream on when you are there.
It is a land.
There are seashells there.
It has sand.
What is it?

Answer: *The beach.*

Faizaan Bharucha (7)
Lever Edge Primary Academy, Bolton

What Is It?

It is a reptile.
This creature lives in the ocean.
It is as green as grass.
It is huge and hates humans.
Its teeth are sharp like a shark's teeth.
What is it?

Answer: A crocodile.

Maira Mahmood (7)
Lever Edge Primary Academy, Bolton

What Am I?

I start with a U and end with an N.
I have a pink or yellow horn.
I have a tail.
I have a pink nose.
My feet are pink.
I don't exist.
What am I?

Answer: A unicorn.

Zahra Azeem (7)
Lever Edge Primary Academy, Bolton

What Am I?

I live in the sea.
I am really mean.
I am grey.
I look silly.
I have one eye on each side of my head.
I look like a hammer.
What am I?

Answer: A hammerhead shark.

Sanah Omar (7)
Lever Edge Primary Academy, Bolton

What Am I?

I am a mammal.
I am big.
I am blue.
I live in the sea.
I love eating fish.
I am the biggest sea animal in the world.
What am I?

Answer: A whale.

Husna Mahamud (7)
Lever Edge Primary Academy, Bolton

What Am I?

I am a reptile.
I can go on land.
I can go in the water.
I have razor-sharp teeth.
I have scales.
I am not nice.
What am I?

Answer: A crocodile.

Ameelia Safaa Mohamed (7)
Lever Edge Primary Academy, Bolton

What Am I?

I give oxygen.
I have petals.
I have a green stem.
I have two leaves.
I need sunlight and water.
I have nectar.
What am I?

Answer: A flower.

Ayaan Mohammed (7)
Lever Edge Primary Academy, Bolton

What Is It?

It spins.
You can stand on it.
You can live on it.
It is big.
It has countries.
It starts with W.
What is it?

Answer: *The world.*

Subhana Ibrahim (7)
Lever Edge Primary Academy, Bolton

What Am I?

I am white.
I am flat.
You can fold me.
I can be ripped.
I am in a book.
I start with a P.
What am I?

Answer: Paper.

Muhammed Ali Omar (7)
Lever Edge Primary Academy, Bolton

What Am I?

I live in the water.
I have nine brains.
I am a mollusc.
I make ink.
I have eight legs.
What am I?

Answer: An octopus.

Hamza Ibrahim (7)
Lever Edge Primary Academy, Bolton

What Am I?

I have windows.
I have a door.
I am tall.
I have stairs.
I have cameras.
What am I?

Answer: A house.

Mohammed-Adam Amir (7)
Lever Edge Primary Academy, Bolton

The Clever Animal

I eat delicious, yummy aphids.
I am red or bright orange and also black.
I am very, very little.
I am so, so cute.
People touch me all the time and play with me.
What am I?

Answer: A ladybug.

Aahana Chawla (6)
Nanaksar Primary School, Hillingdon

The Small Jumper

I live in a big country.
I am a cute mammal.
I have a hard shell that is brown.
I am a herbivore.
I have a pair of small ears.
I hibernate when it's cold.
What am I?

Answer: An armadillo.

Prabaljodh Singh (6)
Nanaksar Primary School, Hillingdon

The Fast Swimmer

It lives in the ocean.
It has eight tentacles.
It likes to eat too much food.
It has two googly eyes.
It begins with an O.
Also, it has a big smile.
What is it?

Answer: An octopus.

Praneesh Southeesan (6)
Nanaksar Primary School, Hillingdon

The Best Hopper

I am very tall.
I hop so high.
I have two long legs.
I have a cute baby.
I have hands to help me hop.
I look like a rabbit but I'm not a rabbit.
What am I?

Answer: A kangaroo.

Dilsheen Nangpal (6)
Nanaksar Primary School, Hillingdon

The Best Surprise Ever

I come in party bags.
People get me on birthdays.
I can be wrapped.
I make people happy.
I come in different shapes.
I have lollipops in me.
What am I?

Answer: A gift.

Sienna Rana (6)
Nanaksar Primary School, Hillingdon

The Scariest Animal

I live in Australia.
I have a long tongue.
I am a carnivore.
I am squeezy.
I live in hot places.
I am any colour.
I am a good hunter.
What am I?

Answer: A snake.

Gurmanbir Singh (6)
Nanaksar Primary School, Hillingdon

The Fastest Runner

I have lots of spots on my body.
I am a carnivore that eats juicy meat.
I like to hunt for my prey.
I live in a hot place.
I can run fast.
What am I?

Answer: A cheetah.

Anaya Chana (6)
Nanaksar Primary School, Hillingdon

The Sea Animal

I live in the blue sea.
I have a hard shell.
I glide in the water.
My skin is green.
I hide in my shell.
I lay lots of eggs.
What am I?

Answer: A turtle.

Arshdeep Singh Bajwa (6)
Nanaksar Primary School, Hillingdon

The Best Eater

I am orange.
I have a long tail.
I eat yummy meat.
I live in Africa.
I have sharp teeth.
I love to run.
I have soft fur.
What am I?

Answer: A lion.

Taranveer Singh (6)
Nanaksar Primary School, Hillingdon

In The Water

I live under the water.
I have sharp teeth.
I eat fish.
I am a carnivore.
I have a tail.
I have a sharp horn on my head.
What am I?

Answer: A narwhal.

Angad Randhawa (6)
Nanaksar Primary School, Hillingdon

The Stripy Creature

I have black and orange stripes.
I have sharp teeth.
I am a carnivore, I eat meat.
I like eating other animals.
I am very rude.
What am I?

Answer: A tiger.

Vinika Kaur (6)
Nanaksar Primary School, Hillingdon

The Beautiful Animal

I am orange and black.
I have two wings.
I live in plants.
I have white spots.
I like to fly.
I love flowers.
What am I?

Answer: A monarch butterfly.

Avneet Gurna (6)
Nanaksar Primary School, Hillingdon

The Scary Animal

I eat tasty fish.
I have very sharp teeth.
I live in England.
My skin colour is dark blue and light blue.
I live in the water.
What am I?

Answer: A shark.

Japji Dhillion (5)
Nanaksar Primary School, Hillingdon

The Animal That Stands On One Leg

I stand on one leg in the water.
I am pink.
I have two big feathers.
I like to be in clear water.
I eat lots of shrimp.
What am I?

Answer: A flamingo.

Ashwika Logeswaran (6)
Nanaksar Primary School, Hillingdon

Wrappers

I am colourful.
I have colourful stripes.
I make people happy.
Sometimes I make people unhappy.
I can be found in the mud.
What am I?

Answer: A gift.

Sahibpreet Singh (6)
Nanaksar Primary School, Hillingdon

Something Powerful

I have so many colours on me.
When the rain comes, I can be seen.
I live in the sky.
When the sun comes, nobody can see me.
What am I?

Answer: A rainbow.

Fateh Singh (6)
Nanaksar Primary School, Hillingdon

The Cutest Animal

I have black and white fur.
I am a herbivore.
I live in China.
I am fluffy.
I fall over a lot.
I have small feet.
What am I?

Answer: A panda.

Bhavik Bhavik (6)
Nanaksar Primary School, Hillingdon

Winter

I come in the winter.
I go on top of your house.
I am not alive.
I can be in your house.
You can eat me.
I can melt.
What am I?

Answer: Snow!

Jugaad Singh Nagpal (6)
Nanaksar Primary School, Hillingdon

Watching Youtube

Everybody watches me every day.
I put so many things on.
Everybody likes to watch me.
Everybody likes to watch YouTube on me.
What am I?

Answer: A TV.

Anaya Sharma (6)
Nanaksar Primary School, Hillingdon

The Venomous Killer

I live in India.
I am venomous.
I have a big head.
I am long.
I have sharp scales.
I can kill people.
What am I?

Answer: A king cobra.

Harshaan Singh (6)
Nanaksar Primary School, Hillingdon

I Am A Long Jumper

I have whiskers.
I have four legs.
I have a fluffy tail.
I am soft.
I have long ears.
I jump very high.
What am I?

Answer: A rabbit.

Vihaan Singh Bansal (5)
Nanaksar Primary School, Hillingdon

The High Jumper

I am a high jumper.
I eat tasty fish.
I like to rest in the sun.
I purr.
I lick my fur.
I am a carnivore.
What am I?

Answer: A cat.

Zorawar Rana (6)
Nanaksar Primary School, Hillingdon

Spotty

It has a long neck and a short tail.
It has long legs and yellow skin.
It has a cute face and dots on its skin.
What is it?

Answer: A giraffe.

Arjun Singh Uppal (6)
Nanaksar Primary School, Hillingdon

Sea Creature

I live in the sea.
Sharks eat me.
I don't eat every day.
I am nice and kind.
I can leap.
What am I?

Answer: A fish.

Japleen Gulati (6)
Nanaksar Primary School, Hillingdon

In The Sea

I eat fish.
I have sharp teeth.
I am extremely dangerous.
I swim in the ocean.
What am I?

Answer: A hammerhead shark.

Jayneev Kapoor (6)
Nanaksar Primary School, Hillingdon

Cold

I am cold.
I love penguins.
I am wet.
I am shivering.
I am white.
I am super cold.
What am I?

Answer: Ice.

Harjun Sira (6)
Nanaksar Primary School, Hillingdon

Hop, Hop!

I am a herbivore.
I like eating fruit and vegetables.
I can be brown, but I am mostly white.
What am I?

Answer: A rabbit.

Harjaap Singh (6)
Nanaksar Primary School, Hillingdon

Cold

I am slippery and white.
I am found in Antarctica.
I am made out of water.
I am very cold.
What am I?

Answer: Ice.

Arjan Singh Mann (6)
Nanaksar Primary School, Hillingdon

In The Sea

I come in different colours.
I live in the sea.
I have a small tail.
I have two fins.
What am I?

Answer: A fish.

Aishleen Kaur (6)
Nanaksar Primary School, Hillingdon

The Rattling Creature

I make a rattling sound.
I have venomous teeth.
I am the fastest slitherer.
What am I?

Answer: A rattlesnake.

Vicram Sandhu (5)
Nanaksar Primary School, Hillingdon

Guess My Riddle

It sounds like the wind blowing the leaves.
It tastes like vinegar apples.
It looks long and leafy.
It smells sweet and tasty.
Its emotion is anger and jealousy.
It makes me feel happy and excited.
What is it?

Answer: An apple tree.

Evnoia Shittu (5)
St Patrick's Catholic Primary School, Birmingham

Guess My Riddle

It smells like the wind.
It feels as soft as a teddy.
It tastes like animal food.
It sounds like *woof!*
It looks like a pillow.
Its emotion is joy.
It makes me feel loved.
What is it?

Answer: A dog.

Ezer Gidey (5)
St Patrick's Catholic Primary School, Birmingham

Guess My Riddle

It smells like popsicles.
It looks so yummy.
It sounds like ice rumbling.
It tastes like ice balls.
Its emotion is surprise.
It makes me feel excited.
What is it?

Answer: An ice castle in Antarctica.

Morireoluwa Olusola (5)
St Patrick's Catholic Primary School, Birmingham

Guess My Riddle

It smells cheesy.
It looks like a triangle.
It sounds like nothing.
It tastes like it is too good to eat.
Its emotion is pride.
It makes me feel hungry.
What is it?

Answer: A pizza.

Zanrae-Xya Arlington-Thompson (5)
St Patrick's Catholic Primary School, Birmingham

Guess My Riddle

It smells fresh.
It looks so fluffy.
It sounds like *miaow, miaow, ssss!*
It tastes bitter.
Its emotion is happiness.
It makes me feel excited.
What is it?

Answer: A cat.

Flourish Midele (5)
St Patrick's Catholic Primary School, Birmingham

Guess My Riddle

It looks soft and cute.
It smells like bubblegum.
It sounds like purring.
It tastes like blood.
Its emotion is happiness.
It makes me feel delighted.
What is it?

Answer: A cat.

Michaela Dede-Bamfo (5)
St Patrick's Catholic Primary School, Birmingham

Guess My Riddle

It is fluffy.
It smells like poop.
It sounds like *woof, woof!*
It tastes like sausages.
Its emotion is happiness.
It makes me feel proud.
What is it?

Answer: A dog.

Joy Segbedzi (5)
St Patrick's Catholic Primary School, Birmingham

Guess My Riddle

She has a fishtail.
She smells like fresh air.
She sounds like music.
She feels smooth.
She tastes magical.
She looks like a sparkly fish.
Who is she?

Answer: A mermaid.

Havya Dhandapani (5)
St Patrick's Catholic Primary School, Birmingham

Guess My Riddle

It smells beautiful.
It looks fluffy and soft.
It sounds squidgy.
It tastes sweet.
Its emotion is happiness.
It makes me feel delighted.
What is it?

Answer: A pizza.

Mateo Ramirez (5)
St Patrick's Catholic Primary School, Birmingham

Guess My Riddle

It smells nice.
It looks hot.
It sounds like sizzling.
It tastes like cheese.
Its emotion is worried.
It makes me feel hungry.
What is it?

Answer: A pizza.

Elijah Ermias (4)
St Patrick's Catholic Primary School, Birmingham

The Fluffy Thing

I'm cute and fluffy and have a small tail,
You could find me on an Aussie trail.
If you see me, you'll want hugs and kisses,
I live in a tree and eat eucalyptus.
People think we're bears, but we're really not,
We live in a country that's really hot!
We're close to kangaroos,
And we really love to snooze.
I hope you get the answer from all these clues.
What am I?

Answer: A koala.

Layla Allen (7)
Westbourne School, Sheffield

The Grassland Hunter

I am a large mammal.
I live in India and I rest all day.
I am sneaky and creep through the long grass to catch my lunch!
My eyes are big and yellow,
And my long tail twitches when I am ready to pounce.
My teeth are as sharp as knives.
My tongue is rough.
I have the mightiest roar!
What am I?

Answer: A tiger.

Florence Smith (7)
Westbourne School, Sheffield

Glowing Amber!

I am as orange as a flame.
I glow like 100 light bulbs.
You can only see me in the evening.
Almost everyone thinks I am beautiful.
It looks like I am on the ground,
But I am not.
I am like a huge orange,
But I am not.
What am I?

Answer: A sunset.

Indu Shastry (8)
Westbourne School, Sheffield

Ground Toucher

I get dirty on the bottom,
And sometimes on the top.
There are different types of me.
I get tighter and tighter when I am pulled.
I can't control myself.
I can come small and tall.
I am kept on racks.
What am I?

Answer: A shoe.

Beatrice Houston (7)
Westbourne School, Sheffield

The Green Thing

I have an ear but can't hear.
I'm yellow and you can peel me,
But I am not a banana.
I'm stacked like bricks,
But you can eat me.
I'm sweet, but I'm not sugar.
I go good with milk.
What am I?

Answer: Corn.

Rafe Dalrymple (7)
Westbourne School, Sheffield

The Mystery

I fly in the sky,
But also stay on the ground.
When I come close to water, I stay dry.
I am as black as ink.
I only appear when the sun is out.
I am everywhere in a haunted house.
What am I?

Answer: A bird's shadow.

Edith Loncaster (7)
Westbourne School, Sheffield

The Night Traveller

My home is somewhere very cold.
I live with my wife.
I have lots of friends who I work with all year round.
Me and my animals work very hard to make people happy.
My vehicle is super fast!
Who am I?

Answer: Santa.

Grace Smith (7)
Westbourne School, Sheffield

The Saviour Of Life

If you're in trouble, call me,
My number is 999.
I work for the Prime Minister and the Queen.
I want to be in control,
I can't quit!
I'm like a superhero.
What am I?

Answer: A police officer.

Zoya Qureshi (7)
Westbourne School, Sheffield

Apex

I live in Asia.
I have four legs.
I am orange.
I am good at climbing trees.
I like to stalk.
I can blend into my surroundings.
I like to live alone.
What am I?

Answer: A tiger.

Malakai Kurpiel-Wang (7)
Westbourne School, Sheffield

Layla's Riddle

I follow you all the time,
I copy your every move.
You can't catch me,
I'm always there.
You can't always see me,
You can't touch me.
What am I?

Answer: Your shadow.

Layla Horton (7)
Westbourne School, Sheffield

Watch Out!

I am the colours of the sun.
I am a good jumper.
I can be sly.
Night-time is when I move.
I am nocturnal.
I love eating loads of things.
What am I?

Answer: A fox.

Lucy Tallis (7)
Westbourne School, Sheffield

A Black Figure

I am as black as the night sky.
I have a black car with boosters.
I only come at night,
And I fight.
I have an enemy.
Who am I?

Answer: Batman.

Zayaan Aslam (7)
Westbourne School, Sheffield

The Burning Flame

I melt when I am lit.
When I'm out, I make lots of smoke.
I am tall when I am young.
I am short when I am old.
What am I?

Answer: A candle.

Patience Schofield (7)
Westbourne School, Sheffield

Something In The Sky

I am colourful.
I am in the sky.
I am bright.
I am cheerful.
I am beautiful.
What am I?

Answer: A rainbow.

Eva Loganathan (7)
Westbourne School, Sheffield

The Fastest Animal Alive

What animal is covered in golden fur
And black spots
And is the fastest land animal?

Answer: A cheetah.

Konstantina Oikonomou (6)
Westbourne School, Sheffield

YOUNG WRITERS INFORMATION

We hope you have enjoyed reading this book – and that you will continue to in the coming years.

If you're a young writer who enjoys reading and creative writing, or the parent of an enthusiastic poet or story writer, do visit our website www.youngwriters.co.uk. Here you will find free competitions, workshops and games, as well as recommended reads, a poetry glossary and our blog.

If you would like to order further copies of this book, or any of our other titles, then please give us a call or visit www.youngwriters.co.uk.

Young Writers
Remus House
Coltsfoot Drive
Peterborough
PE2 9BF
(01733) 890066
info@youngwriters.co.uk